Cryptocurrency Trading : How I made $25000 from $500

+Secret Insider Info only in this book

Donald Fletcher

Table of Contents

Chapter №1: Blockchain Is Revolutionizing The World

Why The Blockchain Will Change The World?

The blockchain is turning into the establishment of quite a bit of your digital life. Also, you likely don't understand it. Blockchain constantly has a changeless "record" that you can perceive, check, and control. In the meantime, it has no single purpose of breakdown from which records or digital resources can be hacked or tainted. As a result of its distributed-ledger innovation, blockchain has applications over each sort of digital record & exchange, and we're as of now observing real businesses inclining toward the move.

Huge business will continuously drive development, and the ascent of blockchain-based smart contracts transforms blockchain into a middleman to carry out all modes of complex business bargains, legitimate understandings, and automated exchanges of information. Simultaneously, loads of startups are utilizing the innovation for everything from worldwide payments to music sharing, from following diamond deals to the lawful marijuana industry. That is the reason blockchain's potential is so huge: When it comes to digital resources & exchanges, you can set totally anything on a blockchain.

A large group of monetary, lawful, administrative, and innovative obstacles must be scaled prior we see across the board reception of blockchain innovation; however primary movers are making staggering steps. Inside the following handful of years, vast swaths of your digital life may start to keep running on a blockchain formation and you may not grasp it.

Blockchain Innovation Will Revolutionize The World

It's my conviction that Blockchain innovation will be as essential to the world as Gutenberg's printing press. Without precedent for the historical backdrop of the world, we can reconsider how the world executes without depending on a liaison. Here are 4 surprising modes the Blockchain may transform the planet, like:

- *Distributed Cloud Storage*

The Blockchain has just been controlled to store data in unscaleable means. A niche storage trick is transmitting the small quantity of Bitcoin to addresses that symbolize data when changed over into a Unicode layout. Other than being a hobby for geeks, Blockchain data storage could be troublesome. Existing cloud storage administrations are brought together along these lines users must place faith in a solitary storage supplier. Through the Blockchain, this can happen to decentralized.

In addition, users can lease their extra storage limit, Airbnb-style, making fresh commercial centers. Bearing in mind the world uses up $22 billion + on cloud storage alone, this could unlock an income stream for normal users, while essentially diminishing the expenditure to store information for organizations and individual users.

- *Unbreakable Contracts*

Smart contracts are arrangements that are self-executing or self-enforcing. The Blockchain's part of the agreement is to restore a third party necessitated to determine a legitimate question. Identified as colored coins or smart properties, a token could be utilized to signify any asset, from stocks to autos. The capacity to hard-code exchange of proprietorship when dealing these assets can conceivably make unbreakable contracts. Rather than confiding in the client or employing a costly legal counselor, the organization could make a smart property through a self-executing contract.

Aforesaid an agreement may resemble this: For each blue gadget delivered, exchange cost per item from the client's bank account to the factory's bank account. Not exclusively does this wipe out the requirement for a deposit or escrow which puts faith in a third party the client is shielded from the factory under-delivering. Despite the fact that this remaining typically hypothesis, platforms such as Ethereum is leading to smart contracts nearer to reality. Moreover, in light of the fact that data stored in the Blockchain can't be fiddled, essential contracts similar to marriages have just been recorded in code.

- *End Of Patents*

Nothing like smart contract platforms, PoE (ProofOfExistence.com) has unleashed fundamental lawful administrations that can be utilized today. As one of the principal non-financial related employments of the Blockchain, PoE stores scrambled data on the Blockchain. This empowers an un-replicable exchange hash to be related with a one of an exclusive record that is put away off the Blockchain. The finest utilize case for this could be replacing patents.

An organization, for example, Apple might need to demonstrate it made an innovation at a specific date without petitioning for a publically-known patent. In the event that anybody challenges its rights for innovation, it could later uncover internal reports that are connected to the exchange hash, subsequently demonstrating presence at the date determined on the Blockchain.

- *Electronic Voting*

The automation of numbering paper votes is an easy decision for the expense, time, and precision enhancements. Nonetheless, past frameworks have been filled with technical issues. The primary issues are the failure to check a machine's precision amid recounts and being key targets for hackers. It is not amazing that political gatherings have officially focused on the Blockchain for their internal voting. The Blockchain is a protected system on the grounds that every exchange is scrambled with a hash that is utilized to check the succeeding hash. Basically, this implies transforming one vote entails a huge number of votes to be changed prior another vote is cast.

The system is ensured by the straightforward truth that no hacker has sufficient computing power to revise such a variety of votes that rapidly. A hacker would really require more computing power than the greatest 500 super-computers consolidated, 256 times over. On the precision front, Blockchain's pseudonymity enables each vote to be publically shared without recognizing the voter. Thus, every voter could check their vote has been tallied from open records. This might one day take out election corruption in the undeveloped world.

What are Blockchain & Cryptocurrencies?

The year 2016 was viewed as the transitioning of Blockchain & cryptocurrencies, with a major ascent in the profile of Blockchain innovation and cryptocurrencies such as Bitcoin & Ethereum.

- *Blockchain*

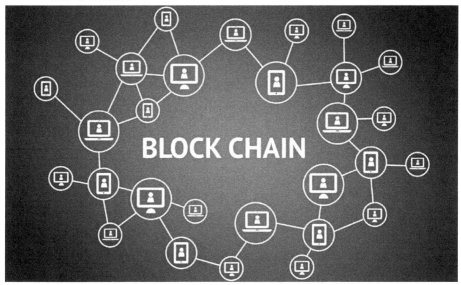

A blockchain is a public record of the entire cryptocurrency exchanges that have ever been performed. It is continually developing as finished blocks are expanded to it with another arrangement of recordings. The blocks are amplified to the blockchain in a straight, chronological order. Every node (PC associated with the Bitcoin system utilizing a client that plays out the task of approving & transferring exchanges) obtains a duplicate of the blockchain, which gets downloaded automatically after joining the Bitcoin framework. The blockchain has finish data regarding the addresses and their balances precisely from the genesis block genesis block to the most lately finished block.

- *Cryptocurrency*

Cryptocurrency is a mode of trade as ordinary monetary forms, for example, USD, however, intended with the end goal of trading digital information via a procedure made conceivable by specific standards of cryptography. Cryptography is utilized to secure the exchanges and to control the formation of fresh coins. The main cryptocurrency to be made was Bitcoin in 2009. Nowadays there are many different cryptocurrencies, frequently declared to as Altcoins. In other words, cryptocurrency is electricity transformed over into lines of code with fiscal esteem. In the understandable of forms, cryptocurrency is digital currency.

The majority of cryptocurrencies are intended to diminish in production over time such as Bitcoin, which makes a market cap on them. That is not quite the same as fiat currencies where budgetary organizations can simply make extra, subsequently inflation. Bitcoin will never have greater than 21 million coins available for use. The technical framework on which all cryptocurrencies depend on was made by Satoshi Nakamoto. Even as several distinctive cryptocurrency specifications exist, nearly all are gotten from one of two protocols; Proof-of-work or the Proof-of-stake. The whole cryptocurrencies are kept up by a group of cryptocurrency miners who are individuals from the overall population that has set up their PCs or ASIC machines to take an interest in the approval and handling of exchanges.

Why This Technology Is Popular Now & Who Are Using That?

The blockchain is presently mounting above the buildup, and numerous inventive utilize cases are developing outside the banking & financing sector plus capital markets too. The imaginative interruption that the innovation will, in the long run, have the capacity to make remains is seen.

The problematic capability of blockchain innovation is, as it, depended on its capacity to build up faith and ease communications in digital ecosystems. With blockchain, the dependability, speed, and perceptibility of exchanges are expanded, together with associations & people are along these lines ready to believe each other in a shared system. The advantages of blockchain for the payments sector are discussed a ton, yet it can change any sort of communications that necessitates making contracts and exchanging worth or data between parties.

Accenture is an affiliate of the Hyperledger Foundation, a consortium devoted to making advanced blockchain innovation. Accenture is likewise active in blockchain usage around the world and put resources into new organizations offering the important blockchain utilize cases to market.

Ripple, a startup business is as of now utilizing blockchain to exchange cross-fringe payments among banks in real-time, and NASDAQ is guiding an answer that decreases the time required for clearing & settling trades. The consistent innovation is utilized far and wide to oversee invoice disputes, trace diamonds, and to store records of academic certificates, just to specify a couple of realistic cases.

Distributed ledgers could still change producing value chains. A new auto could acquire a unique identifier code for a mutual record after assembling. Amid the lifecycle of the vehicle, occasions, for example, possession changes & registrations, maintenance, and mishaps would be refreshed to the record, with the goal that the dependable vehicle history could be ensured whenever, such as when acquiring a used car.

Advantages & Disadvantages

Blockchain typically acknowledged as the backbone innovation behind Bitcoin is one of the hottest plus most fascinating technologies as of now in the marketplace. Given that 2013 Google searches for blockchain have increased 1900%. Like the ascending of the web, blockchain can possibly genuinely upset numerous businesses and make procedures more autonomous, secure, clear, and productive. Startup businesses, entrepreneurs, investors, worldwide associations, and governments have all acknowledged blockchain as a ground-breaking innovation. Below are the advantages & disadvantages of blockchain:

Advantages

- *Disintermediation*

The primary value of a blockchain is that it empowers a database to be straightforwardly shared without a central administrator. Instead of having several centralized application logic, blockchain exchanges have their individual verification of legitimacy & approval to authorize the limitations. Henceforth, with the blockchain going about as an accord component to guarantee the hubs remain in a state of harmony, exchanges can be checked and prepared autonomously.

- *Engage Users*

Users are responsible for all their data & transactions.

- *High-Quality Data*

Blockchain information is absolute, reliable, finely, precise, and broadly accessible.

- *Toughness, Consistency, & Longevity*

Because of the decentralized systems, blockchain doesn't have a midpoint of breakdown and is better up to endure malicious attacks.

- *Process Trustworthiness*

Users can assume that transactions will be performed precisely as the protocol commands evacuating the requirement for a trusted third party.

- *Clearness & Continuity*

Modifications to public blockchains are openly perceptible by all parties making clearness, and all exchanges are unchallengeable, which means they can't be customized or erased.

- *Ecosystem Simplification*

Through all exchanges being added to a solitary public ledger, 4 decreases the messiness & complexities of numerous records.

- *Speedier Transactions*

Interbank exchanges can possibly take days for clearing & final settlement, particularly outside of working hours. Blockchain transactions can diminish exchange times to minutes plus are prepared a day in and day out.

- *Drop Transaction Costs*

By disposing of party mediators and overhead expenses for trading resources, Blockchain can possibly enormously diminish transactions charges.

Disadvantages

- *Execution*

As a result of the idea of blockchains, it will constantly be moderate than centralized databases. At the point when an exchange is being prepared, a blockchain needs to do all similar things simply like a customary database does, yet it holds three extra loads also:

  o *Signature Verification*

Each blockchain exchange ought to digitally sign utilizing a public-private cryptography method, for example, ECDSA. This is fundamental since transactions proliferate among nodes in a peer-to-peer manner, therefore their source can't generally be confirmed. The era & confirmation of these signatures are computationally multifaceted and constitutes the essential bottleneck in products like our own. By dissimilarity, in centralized databases, once an association has been built up, there is no compelling reason to exclusively check each request that approaches over it.

  o *Agreement Instruments*

In a distributed database, such as a blockchain, exertion must be exhausted in guaranteeing that nodes in the system attain accord. Contingent upon the accord component utilized, this may include critical back-and-forth correspondence furthermore additionally managing forks and their ensuing rollbacks. As it's factual that centralized databases should likewise battle with clashing and prematurely ended transactions, these are far more improbable where exchanges are lined and handled in a solitary location.

o *Redundancy*

This isn't about the execution of an individual hub, yet the aggregate sum of calculation that a blockchain requires. While brought together databases process exchanges once (or twice), in a blockchain they should be handled freely by each hub in the system. So parcels more work is being accomplished for a similar final product.

o *Blossoming Technology*

Settling difficulties, for example, transaction speed, the confirmation procedure, and data limits will be vital in making blockchain generally pertinent.

o *Unverifiable Administrative Status*

Since modern currencies have constantly been made & controlled by national governments, blockchain plus Bitcoin confront an obstacle in the broad appropriation by preceding financial organizations if its government direction status stays variable.

o *Large Energy Consumption*

The Bitcoin blockchain systems miners are endeavoring 450 thousand trillion solutions for each second in endeavors to approve transactions, utilizing considerable amounts of PC power.

o *Control, Security, & Protection*

As solutions exist, together with private or permission blockchains and solid encryption, there are still cyber security alarms that should be tended to prior the overall population will endow their own information to a blockchain solution.

o   *Integration Concerns*

Blockchain applications present arrangements that need note-worthy variations too, or finish substitution of, existing frameworks. With a specific end goal to do the switch, organizations should strategize the change.

o   *Social Acceptance*

Blockchain symbolizes a total move to a decentralized system which necessitates the buy-in of its users & administrators.

o   *Expenditure*

Blockchain tenders huge reserves in exchange expenses and time yet the high initial capital expenses could be an obstacle.

Chapter №2: The Extremely Trendy Cryptocoins

For 2014-2017

Analyze Of The Most Popular Cryptocoins For The 2013-2017?

Bitcoin started working in January 2009 and is the primary decentralized cryptocurrency, along with the second digital currency, Namecoin, holding off on developing till over 2 years later in April 2011. At the moment, there are loads of cryptocurrencies with a market value that are being exchanged, and a large number of cryptocurrencies that have existed sooner or later. The universal component of these diverse cryptocurrency frameworks is public ledger or blockchain that is shared amongst network members and the utilization of native tokens as an approach to motivations members for running the system without a central authority. Nonetheless, there are noteworthy contrasts between various cryptocurrencies with respect to the level of development showed.

The bulk of cryptocurrencies is to a great extent clones of Bitcoin or different cryptocurrencies and just components diverse parameter esteems (e.g., distinctive block time, cash supply, plus issuance scheme). These cryptocurrencies indicate next to zero advancements and are frequently alluded to as altcoins. Cases incorporate Dogecoin & Ethereum Classic. Conversely, various cryptocurrencies have developed that, while acquiring a few ideas from Bitcoin, give novel and creative components that present substantive contrasts.

These can incorporate the presentation of new accord systems (e.g., proof-of-stake) and additionally decentralized computing platforms together with smart contract abilities that give significantly unique usefulness and empower nonmonetary usage cases. These cryptocurrency & blockchain innovations can be gathered into two classes: novel (public) blockchain frameworks that trait their own particular blockchain (e.g., Ethereum, Zcash, Peercoin), in addition to dApps/other that exist on extra layers based on existing blockchain frameworks. There are over 5000 cryptocurrencies on the planet yet we've shortlisted the Top CryptoCoins traded by market cap, demand, future span plus value investment asset.

Top Cryptocoins Traded For The 2013-2017Are:

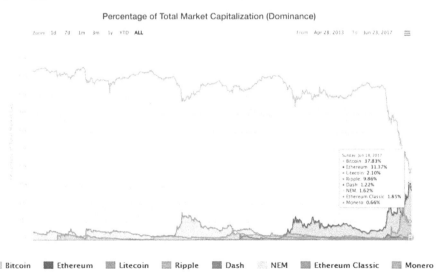

Percentage of Total Market Capitalization (Dominance)

Source: coinmarketcap.com

- *Bitcoin*

Not surprisingly, the Bitcoin is the highest priority on the rundown with a market capitalization of $29,919,930,192. It was designed by Satoshi Nakamoto at the time; it was the main virtual money accessible in the market and it's the pricey virtual currency in the market acknowledged & legitimized in numerous nations.

- *Ethereum (ETH)*

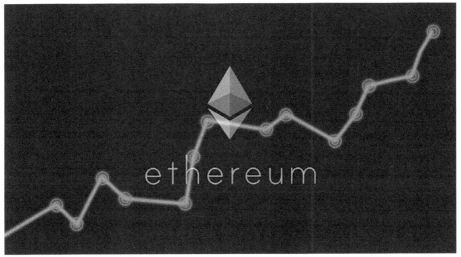

Ethereum is the most well known and proficient cryptocurrency presented in the year 2013, which is open-source, decentralized & productive world computing platform which has numerous extra functionalities, for example, Smart contracts & EVM (Ethereum Virtual Machine). 30+ worldwide brands such as Microsoft, JP Morgan Chase, and so forth have begun the EEA (Enterprise Ethereum Alliance) which lights up the eventual fate of the Ethereum blockchain. Ethereum has a swift transaction speed also permits 25 transactions for every second. In the rundown of Poloniex trade, ETH/BTC match is at the top spot with the estimation of ETH as 0.08859 BTC.

- *Litecoin (LTC)*

Litecoin is an open source & P2P (Peer-to-Peer) cryptocurrency. It is decentralized also isn't overseen by any central authority. It was based on the premise of Bitcoin yet has numerous enhancements contrasted with Bitcoin. LTC's real leverage is the Segregated Witness that aides in expanding the exchange speed. Utilizing this algorithm, BTC can have its most noteworthy disadvantage revised. LTC is one more coin exchanged the Poloniex platform which has a cost of 0.01894 BTC.

- *Ripple (XRP)*

Ripple is the speediest & best adaptable digital resource, which empowers real time payments and exchanges doable from anyplace on the planet. It's steady in the market and it is based on an open source blockchain network. In this way, it gives all the components of Blockchain. They permit truly quick transactions which just take 4 seconds. Also, they permit just about 1000 exchanges for each second which is immensely higher than any driving cryptocurrency. In the Poloniex trade, the XRP has a cost of 0.00008256 BTC and for the XRP/BTC match; the volume in 24 hours is XRP 63,381,380.90 & BTC 5,085.34.

- *Dash*

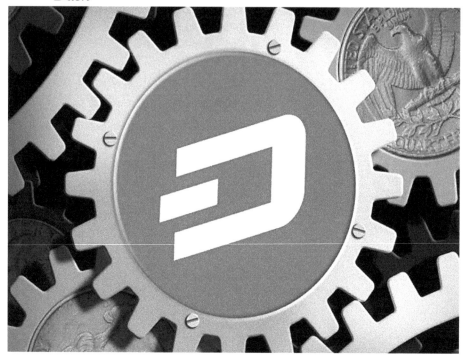

Dash is a cryptocurrency you can utilize to spend anyplace on the planet. Its transactions are extremely secure and are affirmed by 1,000 Gigahash of X11 ASIC computing power as well as more than 4,100 servers facilitated far and wide. You can send instant payments via the platform and all the information with respect to the individual plus record is detained private by the PrivateSEnd framework. It is totally based upon an open P2P (Peer-to-Peer) network.

- *NEM (XEM) - Distributed Ledger Technology*

NEM is an open source P2P cryptocurrency circulated in 2015 with numerous extra components from the customary blockchain innovation. It was emitted in Java & C++ versions. It presents another algorithm recognized as the PoI (Proof-of-Importance) and multi-sig accounts. It tenders high security to the information stored. The cryptocurrency of the platform is the XEM.

- *Ethereum Classic (ETC)*

Ethereum exemplary is an endeavor to keep the Ethereum blockchain in place on the premise of the fork when DAO appeared & impacted. ETC began exchanging Poloniex and they are acquiring more & more accomplishment from that. The platform is worked from decentralized, permissionless & secure blockchain. Lately, ETC has presented the Die Hard Fork, which counteracts the trouble confronted in the Ethereum blockchain. Right now, the ETC/BTC combine in Poloniex trade has the most recent volume of ETC 468,517.94 & BTC 3,508.35.

- *Monero (XMR)*

Monero is an open source decentralized cryptocurrency got from the Bitcoin which offers importance to security, decentralization, & scalability. It is assembled in view of the crypto note protocol. It ticks off the Proof-of-Work agreement. Monero supplies security in three ways to be specific ring signatures, ring CT, & Stealth addresses. It doesn't have a vigorously coded maximum block size which facilitates in enhancing scalability.

How They Were Growing?

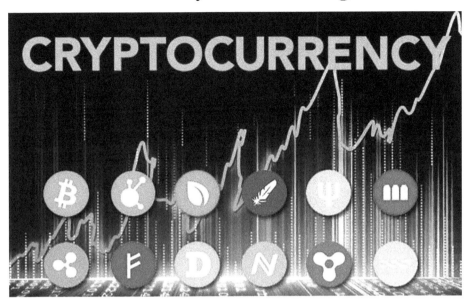

In spite of huge advancement in economic globalization, the worldwide financial framework is still extremely divided, with just a couple of players having an incitement to sit at the table along with the big boys. It is apparent that blockchain can possibly combine and, maybe, even institutionalize financial markets everywhere throughout the world. Different private endeavors & controllers have just begun the voyage of coordinating blockchain into their business models.

Latest forceful climbs in costs of cryptocurrencies are both stirring & concerning. Retail financial investors are extremely energized, while observers are sitting tight for the green light from the expansive institutional players. Fans are foreseeing the new, decentralized, self-representing future, as fundamentalists are searching for certainties behind the hyped-up and indecently high valuations in this circle.

Though, the achievement of cryptocurrencies has likewise implied that new digital monetary standards are consistently being presented. Starting last July, more than 900 cryptocurrencies were accessible for buy over the web. That is countless of needles in the sheaf. In any case, a couple of cryptocurrencies emerge from the group in light of their size. We should investigate the biggest digital currencies by market cap starting in July 2017, as per CoinMarketCap.com, for example,

- *Ethereum: $15.24 billion*
- *Bitcoin: $32.29 billion*
- *Dash: $999.6 million*
- *Zcash: $285.8 million*
- *Ethereum Classic: $1.41 billion*
- *Decred: $132 million*
- *Ripple: $5.89 billion*
- *Litecoin: $2.18 billion*
- *NEM: $903.8 million*
- *Monero: $441.7 million*

In general, the eventual fate of cryptocurrencies appears to be brilliant. Together with 3 million v clients and numbering, organizations across the country may soon support them as payment modes. Philanthropies will have greater adaptability with donations, and pupils will have more choices to pay for school. With respect to the eventual fate of the U.S. dollar, the truth will surface eventually.

Capitalization

Cryptocurrencies are a type of cash particularly intended to exploit the design of the web. Rather than depending on a standard financial establishment to ensure and check exchanges, cryptocurrency transactions are ensured, or "affirmed," by the PCs of the clients on the cash's system. The PCs that check the exchanges ordinarily get a tiny sum of money as an incentive. The course toward accepting incentives in return for confirming incentive is known as mining, and it is the principle course that new cash is created. Mining works distinctively for various monetary standards.

Since cryptocurrencies are totally digital they can be utilized as a part of ways that conventional monetary standards can't; fundamentally, they are utilized as the digital equivalent of money. Not at all like credit or debit cards that are issued by banks, you needn't bother with an account or great credit to utilize cryptocurrencies, nevertheless, you can utilize them to purchase goods and services from an inevitably assorted assortment of retailers & people. For example, Overstock.com and Newegg.com acknowledge Bitcoin as payment. There is normally a little charge for roughly every exchange, except it's commonly much lesser than credit card processing fees also interest, in addition to the expenses support the system.

Cryptocurrencies can be changed over at a lightning velocity or used to symbolize things that aren't typically monetary standards, for example, domain names or purchaser merchandise. Contingent upon the money being utilized, it is likewise probable to anonymize exchanges, transforming cryptocurrencies into a type of discreet online cash. Above all, cryptocurrencies can be sent anyplace on the planet, immediately, empowering clients to bargain straightly with each other over the web, as opposed to through a third-party monetary establishment, paying currency conversion charges or sitting tight for a bank to release funds.

Cryptocurrency's market capitalization is the aggregate worth of all coins at present available for use. A high market capitalization can show a high esteem for every coin or basically a considerable measure of accessible coins. Maybe more vital than market capitalization is day by day trading volume: the estimation of the coins that trade hands each day. A high every day exchanging volume in respect to the market capitalization demonstrates a sound economy with numerous transactions. Cryptocurrencies are an energizing new improvement in the realm of the fund. Nobody is very certain yet where the innovation will lead, however, the reality remains that these new monetary forms offer conceivable outcomes that customary money can't.

What Technologies They Use?

Cryptocurrencies, for example, Bitcoin are a type of digital cash. The fundamental idea was first proposed in 2008 by an anonymous maker and the principal working version was produced as open source software in 2009. Cryptocurrencies empower elective monetary structures that assist worldwide exchanges without the requirement for a bank. Cryptocurrencies depend on a distributed computerized ledger that operates as a digital book keeper & accountant turned into one. They permit clients who don't recognize or believe each other to consequently monitor who claims what.

The compound architecture supporting them was intended to keep financial exchanges from being controlled, making it awfully troublesome for the scam to happen. This innovation has bunches of potential usages beyond banking. It's currently feasible to utilize the blockchain as a database that keeps a wide range of records in a protected and effectively reachable place without arduous, paper-heavy procedures. For now, more than

90 banks around the world, including HSBC & Deutsche Bank, are investigating the capability of the blockchain.

The distributed ledger innovation behind any cryptocurrency, its blockchain, as much all the more convincing. The blockchain is a type of web where the servers & databases are not claimed and worked by huge telecommunications organizations but rather these are decentralized and, as Napster, it is a peer-to-peer innovation. It is fundamentally not subject to a middle man but rather looks like a marketplace where miners/makers (the individuals who utilize their PCs to run the cryptographic calculations which compensate them with tokens/coins on effective finish) and clients (the individuals who expend tokens for transactional reasons and, doubtfully, a store of wealth) execute specifically with each other. This element alone can aid dodge the real issues spinning around the move to de-hazard banks which work in the Caribbean once two occasions happen: the access of extra market players, and far reaching acknowledgment of the innovation by governments & controllers.

A blockchain, in basic terms, is an exceptionally safe and anonymous ledger that gives makers & customers of the token the means, much the same as RTGS (the real time gross settlement) and SWIFT transmission technologies in banking, to encourage cryptocurrency exchanges without the utilization of a middleman, similar to a central bank. Note that RTGS & SWIFT rely upon a direct verification framework utilized by few partners. This presently prompts bottlenecks bringing about the throttling of transactions/wires particularly inside and from tiny financial jurisdictions.

The Top List Of Cryptocurrencies For 2017-2018! The Secret InsiderInfo

With more than 1300 cryptocurrencies (and tallying!), it's to a great degree hard to foresee which ones will wind up on top. Considering the speed at which a large portion of these coins have developed in an incentive in the course of recent months, it's apparent that we are entering an air pocket like that of the dotcom boom This means while loads of these coins will lose the greater part of their incentive in the following 3 years, there will be a chosen few that will turn out to end up easily recognized names such as Google, Apple, IBM, and Microsoft did. Thus how would we discover which ones are the best cryptocurrency to put resources into as per July 2017 data? By choosing them in view of their future potential:

Top List Of Cryptocurrencies For 2017-2018

Bitcoin
Launched In: 2009

Price: $2023.56

Current Market Capitalization: $33.29 billion

All Time High: $2791.70

Ripple
Launched In: 2012

Price: $0.14

Current Market Capitalization: $5.71 billion

All Time High: $0.39

Ethereum
Launched In: 2015

Price: $166.46

Current Market Capitalization: $15.54 billion

All Time High: $407.10

Litecoin
Launched In: 2011

Price: $40.56

Current Market Capitalization: $2.13 billion

All Time High: $56.03

Monero
Launched In: 2014

Price: $32.61

Current Market Capitalization: $476 million

All Time High: $61.69

MaidSafe
Launched In: 2006

Price: $0.27

Current Market Capitalization: $121.13 million

All Time High: around $0.5

Dash
Launched In: 2014

Price: $140.91

Current Market Capitalization: $1.047 billion

All Time High: $225

Steem
Launched In: 2016

Price: $0.96

Current Market Capitalization: $230.44 million

All Time High: $4.34

Siacoin
Launched In: 2015

Price: $0.006

Current Market Capitalization: $177 million

All Time High: around $0.015

Factom
Launched In: 2015

Price: $13.36

Current Market Capitalization: $116.93 million

All Time High: $36.51

Cryptocurrency as an investment alternative is by all accounts rising exponentially. Apparently, the numbers positively are. Generally, cryptocurrency has been pulling in the same number of investors as gold, real estate or penny stocks, if not more. It can be an exceptionally beneficial venture in the event that one recognizes the best cryptocurrency to contribute. Also, this being the era of the web, the chart can just ever move upward.

Chapter №3: How I Made My First $25000? (A Secret Revealed About Cryptocurrencies)

Envision you get up one day, and you have got $25,000 in your account. You didn't put any hard work to gain them nor did you get a legacy from an obscure relative. You've quite recently made a little investment that expanded into a fortune after some time. That is the thing that transpired to me one day!

I'm Donald Fletcher and I live in a residential community Mystic, CT, USA. The aggregate populace of my town is 4,205 and this curious coastline town brags the country's biggest maritime museum as well as some genuinely eye-catching ocean views. I'm a student of University of New Haven (New London Campus). I will share an individual mystery of getting rich while investing a modest amount on cryptocurrencies, for example, Etherium, Bitcoin, Dash, Zcash, Decred, Stratis, Ripple, Neo and so forth? Additionally, did you realize that putting resources into cryptocurrencies could make you a millionaire? That is the manner by which I transformed 500$ into 25,000$.

In 2015, I've learned about Bitcoin while dealing with a task about encryption. The whole framework enthralled me, so I've chosen to invest $500.I disregarded the venture until at some point later when Bitcoin began flying up in the news. Along these lines, I looked at my encrypted wallet just to find that I was sitting on a $25,000 nest egg. Sadly, not every one of you is as fortunate as me. However, that doesn't mean you can't in any way, shape or form turn into a millionaire by putting resources into virtual currency. You simply need to see how they function with the goal that you can boost your benefits.

This inclusive content will show you all that you have to think regarding why you ought to put resources into cryptocurrencies, such as, Etherium, Bitcoin, Dash, Zcash, Decred, Stratis, Ripple, Neo and so on? What's more, how to do it! I will be shortest and tell you that I am not a monetary counselor and put resources into cryptocurrencies at your own particular risk. Let start then, shall we!

Why Will Cryptocurrencies (Etherium, Bitcoin, Dash, Zcash, Decred, Stratis, Ripple, Neo and so on) Make You a Millionaire?

Purchasing virtual currencies may appear like excessively of a hazard. On the contrary, if you reflect with reference to it for a moment, it's one of the flawless investments you could make. Suppose if you had taken the chance and purchased $100 worth of Bitcoin in 2015 at $429 per Bitcoin. Presently it would be worth $423,107 at $ 4,231 per Bitcoin. At the same time, as you can't turn back time and, much the same as myself, spend a couple of bucks on Bitcoin and get up well off two years after the fact, you can in any case profit putting resources into cryptocurrencies at this moment because of:

- *The Worth Of The Us Dollar Is Devalued*

Have you ever ask why you just can't extend your dollars enough any longer? The clarification is fairly straightforward: the estimation of the US dollar is declining. Until 1914 the US dollar had a settled esteem. For instance, on the off chance that you spared ten dollars in 1790, you could even now purchase a similar quantity of products with your reserve funds 100 years after the fact. These days, nonetheless, cash is by all accounts worth less and less consistently.

As time passed by, the paper money supply extended quicker than the nation's gold supply, as well as the US dollar rapidly lost its value. The additional money printed; the more insignificant it turns out to be. Furthermore, this pattern proceeds. As the U.S. determinedly obliterates the estimation of the dollar by overprinting, remote countries are losing trust in the dollar and its part as reserve money.

- *Worldwide Enterprises Award Bitcoin & Ethereum Stamps Of Approval*

One of the greatest organizations on the planet is gambling on virtual currencies. IBM has declared an assortment of organizations along with activities identified with the blockchain. As indicated by an IBM report, 15% of the banks overviewed plan to utilize blockchain by 2017 while 91% of them are as of now putting resources into blockchain for deposit-taking. Finance isn't the main open door IBM sees with blockchain. The organization trusts that the innovation could transform the world.

In any case, IBM isn't the main huge organization inspired by blockchain innovation. Microsoft multiplied down on Ethereum with another blockchain item, the Ethereum Consortium Blockchain Network, a venture that goes for facilitating enterprises cooperate to assemble progressively complex consortia that would use the system impacts of shared, incontrovertible ledgers. Basically, this consortium will enable groups of organizations to send a private Ethereum Network with a solitary click.

- *Virtual Currencies Could Be Substitutions for Gold*

It may be difficult to accept, yet it's a genuine probability, considering that Bitcoin is currently worth greater than gold.

Interestingly, the cost of one Bitcoin has outperformed the cost of one ounce of gold. The vast majority of the early adopters guaranteed that Bitcoin would in the end swap gold as the favored option store of significant worth. On the off chance that it didn't occur up till now, it isn't on account of Bitcoin does not have the ability to wind up noticeably the new gold standard on the contrary since it's still fairly confounded to put resources into the digital currency. It's unstable cost is another feature that made it hard for Bitcoin to wind up noticeably a solid option resource. Yet, now that one Bitcoin is worth larger than one ounce of gold, it could be an indication that it could equal gold as a safe-haven.

- *How To Begin Investing in Bitcoin, Ethereum, & Other Cryptocurrencies*

There are numerous approaches to put resources into virtual currencies, in addition to everything relies upon what you need. Here are the nuts & bolts of purchasing and putting resources into Bitcoin, Ethereum and other substitute cryptocurrencies (altcoins).

o *Coinbase*

In case you're new to digital currencies, at that point, Coinbase is an ideal approach to begin. Coinbase is an online trade platform for exchanging, purchasing, offering, as well as storing cryptocurrencies. Its makers needed to build up an open framework that would enable individuals to change over digital money into their local currency.

o *GDAX & Gemini*

In the event that you've already tried things out and chose that Bitcoin is something worth putting resources into, at that point you have to figure out how to utilize GDAX & Gemini. Much the same as Coinbase, they are trade exchanging platforms that enable you to purchase, offer, and store cryptocurrencies. On the other hand, these frameworks are more multifaceted than Coinbase in addition to ideal for day trading. What is more, they have brought down exchange expenses than Coinbase.

o *Poloniex & Bittrex*

Suppose the gold rush for profiting on Bitcoin as well as Ethereum is finished, what would one be able to do? No compelling reason to stress, there are various little virtual monetary standards, less acknowledged, that is really on the rise quicker than Bitcoin and Ethereum. As a general rule, Bitcoin is the 800-pound gorilla in the room and all other non-Bitcoin monetary standards are alluded to as Altcoins. In the event that you make a head over Coin Market Cap, you can observe a rundown of 100 cryptocurrencies. Comprising of Bitcoin, they all aggregate up to an incredible $28 billion dollar market cap. As it was, many people are taking their risks at these currencies.

o *Coinmarketcap*

It's pretty useful site for getting the up-to-date info's regarding cryptocurrencies market capitalizations, assets, biggest gainers & losers and so on so forth prior investing.

Clutching Bitcoin intends to have an offer in this venture. In the event that Bitcoin ever substitutes monetary reserves of central banks or turns into the prevailing currency for global exchanges only to name two illustrations the estimation of one Bitcoin will be long ways past 10,000 Dollar. Purchasing and keeping cryptocurrencies is a gamble on the accomplishment of this quiet transformation of money. It resembles a safety of a substantial ecosystem. Previously, investors in cryptocurrencies have been absurdly effective. Seeing as 2011, Bitcoin created an expansion in the estimation of no less than 25,000%. And since May 2016, Ethereum esteem shot up by 2,700%. That is perhaps the quickest rally a digital money at any point illustrated. What's more, discussing all cryptocurrencies the total market cap took off by 10,000% since mid-2013.

Would You Be Able to Confide In An Asset, Which Exhibited This Mind Blowing Vertical Take-Off? Should It Not Be A Bubble?

Beyond any doubt: it would have been exceptional to invest one year back, two years prior or six years prior. In any case, on the off chance that you comprehend the capability of likewise be found and if your confidence in their illusion of money, nowadays may be the greatest day doable to begin putting resources into it. We have to take note of that cryptocurrencies are not a typical investment. The unpredictability terribly surpasses that of some other investment group. It is to a few sections unregulated. There is the hazard that cryptocurrencies get prohibited, that trades get hacked or that you drop your digital currency key. Cryptocurrencies are a speculative investment.

Various Vital Tips for Investing In Cryptocurrencies

- *Purchase all that you have confidence in. Also, stay up with the latest on them.*
- *Clutch it for 3mo-1yr, as well as purchase on mega dumps.*
- *When you are up 200-300%, offer your primary investment. Believe me.*
- *Purchase More, Grasp More.*
- *Oh yeah and remember to continue increasing your coins, utilizing steemit for instance!*
- *Crypto is a Bullish market in general, keeping in mind that people, FIAT is fading before our eyes.*

With individuals losing confidence in the conventional banking framework, virtual currencies are starting to be converted into a supplementary tempting choice for both customers as well as organizations. Along these lines, it should not shock anyone that Bitcoin is expanding in esteem, in addition, to being even viewed as a steadfast option to the gold standard. Ethereum, one more open-source, blockchain-based platform is picking up footing as well. More current than Bitcoin, Ethereum concentrates on something new: it's not just with reference to payments in electronic money; it's likewise in relation to the formation of smart contracts. In this manner, as Bitcoin is a digital currency, Ethereum is a platform for streaming applications on a distributed network.

The cause there's such a major buildup around Bitcoin in company with Ethereum is basic. Individuals are burnt out on entrusting their important data, regardless of whether we're discussing currency or information, to a solitary huge organization. Nothing like conventional frameworks, both Bitcoin as well as Ethereum are decentralized, implying that you can utilize them without including an intermediate. You have command over the whole procedure. There is scarcely whenever or outskirt restriction since these platforms and the currencies they are utilizing are widespread. Bitcoin along with Ethereum can give huge favorable circumstances, particularly in the present socioeconomic certainties.

On the other hand, remember that this content isn't by any mean planned to be utilized as financial counsel. I'm not a financial advisor. I am only an active member who has Bitcoin and cryptocurrencies in my investment portfolio with a bullish attitude toward its future. What's more, I need to impart this to you since I trust it's the sort of data we would all be able to profit by one day.

In spite of the fact that I am not a money related counsel, one thing is clear to me: Bitcoin, Ethereum, and other cryptocurrencies are the up-to-the-minute gold rush. Thus, don't get left at the rear! At this time is your opportunity to develop into a millionaire. On the off chance that later than perusing this content and some other expert resources you chose to put resources into virtual currencies, I suggest you begin with Coinbase. As I as of now clarified, it's straightforward to utilize, safe, in addition to free.

Future Crypto Trading Academy or How to make from 15% to 25% per month

The universe of digital money is moving truly quick. In the course of recent years, Bitcoin outflank some other investment such as gold, the stock market or real estate. In excess of the previous year's several new digital currencies turn up on the market. A good number of them are simply impersonator or just have a couple of elements that make them unique. Just a modest bunch of those crypto currencies are genuine aberrations.

The company that I decided to talk about is not just an investment company. **Future crypto trading academy** - It's a community of people who offer to everyone to learn everything about how the crypto currency market works, what nuances there are, and how to entrust its funds to companies that are insured by the English fund to protect investors' rights and Receive stable from 15% to 30% per month every month in the Bitcoin crypto currency.

Let's now take a closer look at how you can become a member of the community and start earning from today.

The first thing you need to do absolutely to any participant is to register in the project at this link

- **https://fct.academy/promo?ref=8OJ4Gzpg**

In the bottom of the photo where you need to click -

The second thing you need to do is pass a simple registration in the community as shown below in the photo -

Sign up

Sign in to enter

@MISSING: app.   FOR
LANGUAGE en-US Here you will see your Sponsor Email
                (my first leverl partner)
Email

Password

☐ I agree with the conditions agreements

Sign Up

Third, you are now an active partner of the company and you are immediately available to three products of the company. -

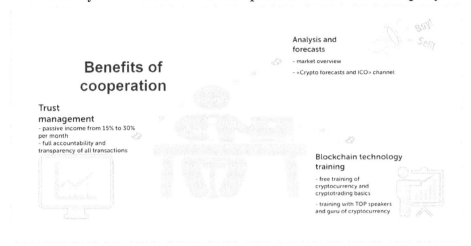

Conclusion

So, after reading this book you can see that world financial market is under the greatest changes. Blockchain technology is something that would bring The application of blockchain technology could take the modernization of the stock market one step further. Instead of technology being used simply to speed up more complex transactions, the blockchain could change how the plumbing behind the system works to mitigate current risks and problems.

While blockchain's best-known, most used and highest-impact application is Bitcoin, the potential impact of the technology is much greater and wider than virtual currencies. Indeed, since other applications can 'piggyback' the Bitcoin blockchain, the biggest impacts of Bitcoin may be found outside the currency domain. Transactions of any kind are usually faster and cheaper for the user when completed via a blockchain, and they also benefit from the protocol's security. Whereas transactions in between some countries are often fast, cheap and secure enough for most purposes, users and proponents of blockchain applications often see additional benefits in its transparency and immutability. Indeed, there is a growing trend towards less trust in financial and governance institutions and greater social expectations of accountability and responsibility. The popularity of Blockchain technology and of other cryptocurrencies may also reflect an emerging social trend of all transactions being cheap, fast and transparent. That is why for now cryptomarket is considered to be one of the highest priority tool for investments nowadays. Cryptocurrencies are not just money, this is our future

Remember: the wealth can be reached with making of certain amounts of right steps. You can make today your first step in your own road to success.

Thank you for taking your time to read this book. I really hope you have a clear vision of cryptocurrency and its market, and and also Blockchain technology.

In addition you also got two sources that can help you to make more money this year or start to invest for the long term. So, this is insider info for investment into cryptocurrencies for 2017, and the new FCT academy that can provide you stable monthly profit and additional knowledge and skills for cryptotrading.

CPSIA information can be obtained
at www.ICGtesting.com
Printed in the USA
LVHW02s2134231217
560697LV00034B/1594/P